# for me(n)

Author:

Constantly straddling the line between an ironic
Instagram artiste and an outspoken social activist, Sophie
Lau enjoys writing about her experiences going through
life as a British Asian woman. Prose, verse, Instagram
highlights reel - she's tried it all!

More often than not, she can be found crying in her
home surrounded by eczema cream and antihistamines,
stressing over her triple honours languages degree and
mildly paralysed by her fear of the future.

She can be found on Instagram at @lenaanus or at
thereformedflake.com

Illustrator:

@nat.akinyi on Instagram
natakinyi.art

# for me(n)

Sophie Lau

illustrations by Nat Akinyi

to sof,
thank you.
you've always shown me unconditional love and support and i
don't think i could have, or would have, published this without
you. since we first met five years ago, you've helped me grow so
much as a person and you've been by my side for every journey
i've taken, creative or otherwise. despite the oceans that now
separate us, i have no doubt that we'll stay just as close as ever,
forever. i'm so so lucky to have gotten to know your soul

to nat,
thank you.
you truly brought my vision to life. as an illustrator, you went
above and beyond what i could have ever conceived! more than
that though, you hold such an important place in my world.
over the past decade, you've always been there (wild, right? a
decade? already??). sometimes a quiet presence, sometimes a
burning star, whichever form you may take, you're an amazing
artist and an even better human. i'm just so so grateful to share
the universe with you

to mummy and daddy,
thank you.
你們是全世界最好的父母。我知道我小時候，很多時後會
不聽你們的話，我也都有小小不乖。事實上我不知道怎麼
寫很多中文字來表達我想說的話，但是我想説，多謝你們
為我做的一切，我希望你們知道我真的很愛你。

to every single person reading this,
thank you.
you reading this lil collection really does mean the world to me.
i hope you enjoy my ramblings and i hope you learn something
valuable - whether it's about relationships, desire, love, or most
important of all, about yourself
(i also hope you don't turn me into a twitter meme)

# a map of my heart

buried demons
or
the one i never loved

**L**

the reason i cried on another boy's bed

i don't think you know
do you
what really happened that night
between movies and jokes and food and
my sheets.

how could you?
i never told anyone
not even myself.

push it all down -
the regret
the shame
the guilt
the tears.

just keep it all down and

tell yourself it doesn't matter.

4

**L**

consequential

you greeted me like
you weren't responsible for
breaking my trust
breaking my heart
breaking my mind

funny, isn't it?
funny how you can move on
ignore everything that happened but
ignoring it gets me nowhere

# D

**D**

we never were good at endings

before there was us, there was her.
i never worried all that much -
the past exists so that we cherish the present
or so i told myself.
you cherished memories and so did i
but i cherished ours and
you
you cherished yours.

we were both guilty, i guess, of living in the past but
guilty was ok
for a while.

you had a cockatoo who never slept and
in the time it took for us to fade
the sun had set and risen again.
do you remember?

even now i foolishly cling on
while you've already let go.
i wish i would have known you were so bad at goodbyes.

i'm bad at them too.

**D**

toxic

i'm wrapped up in the idea of you while
you're wrapped up in her arms

wasted passion
or
the one i loved superficially

**T**

everything we were looking for

with roaming hands and roaming hearts
we pressed ourselves together

you lost yourself in me
and
i found myself in you

**T**

right swipes and regret

i asked you a question once -
you probably don't remember
you probably don't care
you never did care much.

i smiled softly, indulgently, cut you off but
the shadows had entered the growing
          space
between        us and
i knew the end before it came.

i never understood you
the cadence of your voice blending seamlessly into the air
which smelt of regret.

you never saw me
dark hair wrapped around your fist
smudged make-up around slanted eyes
easily transferrable to another fantasy.

**T**

cyclical

i don't blame you for treating me like
i'm disposable
it's the only way either of us know
how to play this game.

bad communication and
missed opportunities but
when you're with me
it never feels like we're pretending.

sure
you waltz in and out of my life
like i'm the entrance to your childhood home
never meant for more than brief respite.

there are memories on my lips and
warmth in my eyes and
you feel whole when you hold me
don't you?

but inevitably
you'll leave.

you'll shut the door and
you'll bury your feelings like you do your insecurities but
it's ok
i understand

it's the only way we know how to be.

**T**

unanswered

you ask me
what i want in life

you ask me
what i want from you

what is it you want to hear?

it's like
we're pretending to be who we were when we first met
but

we don't know how to anymore.

**T**

what's in a name? everything.

i look at that picture sometimes
the one of you and her.

my friend sent it to me one night -
i was drunk and everything i touched and tasted
reminded me of my past mistakes.
i squinted at my phone and
wondered how i should feel.

she's pretty, i guess
in that way you would like.
it makes me wonder -
was i ever attractive in your eyes?

i don't know her name but
that's not the point, is it?
the point is you probably say it
the way you never said mine.

i always wondered what my name would sound like
falling
from
your
lips

i guess i'll never know.

**T**

a learning process

when i learnt how to love myself
i unlearnt how to love you

*a beautiful nightmare*
*or*
*the one i loved forcedly*

**E**

free-falling

i didn't fall in love with you
or at least
that's not how i would describe it

i think i
        plummeted
but you didn't care enough
to catch me

**E**

tears & tears

you held me once
when my tears stained your shirt
like his touch stained my body.

you told me it didn't matter but
i could hear his voice -
he once said the exact same thing.

"it doesn't matter"
"just this once"
"please don't tell her"

you meant it differently
i know
but i couldn't distinguish the gap
between past and
present
between truth and
lie
between you and
him.

so i cried as i felt my mind tear.

**E**

what you couldn't say

i asked
"what are you scared of?"
you never replied

now i know
your biggest fear was
letting me in

**E**

bloody fingertips

splinters of your broken soul are
embedded.
in. my. heart.

how do i dig them out?

**E**

haunted

whenever i close my eyes
i remember that winter morning

i could taste the frost in the air
everything was crisp, clean, raw

i can't recall every detail
it was too long ago and i've stopped torturing myself by
rehashing and remembering and regretting

but
that doesn't mean i don't still feel it

i wish i didn't still feel it

**E**

unexpected, uncontrollable

i would never have guessed
it would hurt more once you'd left.

i don't miss you though
that would be the definition of self-destructiveness and
i've come too far to
fall
        into
that
        spiral.

it's just
everything still reminds me of you.

for a while, i thought i missed you.
i thought i missed the smell of your shirts
the curve of your lips
the timbre of your voice.

you had this way about you and
i felt safe.

i wasn't, of course.

there's nothing safe about memorable scents
about smirking lips
about loaded words whispered into the pitch-black night.

i don't know how i ever thought otherwise.

**E**

never quite whole

for a fraction of a moment
i saw a future.

it wasn't necessarily ours
i'm not sure anything ever really belonged to just us
no matter how much i wanted it to.

there were moments, though
weren't there?
perfect, precious moments that i wanted to live in forever
and sometimes
i think you wanted that too.

but you never did want to commit to anything
least of all, me
so fractions were all we ever had.

**E**

playing pretend

i remember when i thought we were real.
call it blissful ignorance or hopeful naivety
whatever it was
it worked.

i pretended i was happy and
pretending was enough.

i think it was enough for the both of us.

**E**

we need to let go

strange, isn't it?
the way we hold on to each other long after
there's nothing there.

they say
absence makes the heart grow fonder
and
time heals all wounds.

which is it really?

it's just
i keep hoping and waiting
and giving up but staying -

i wish i knew how to stop.

*chosen heartache*
*or*
*the one i loved in order to forget*

**D**

the wonders of the universe can't compare

if i could paint the galaxies that appear in your eyes
if i could capture the stardust that spills from your mouth

i'd have the whole cosmos in my hands

**D**

of the nights i want to remember

i saw constellations painted onto your skin and
soft moonlight shone from your eyes.
the leaves rustled in the whispers that
fell from your lips and

i was utterly enamoured.

your mouth tasted like morning dew
lingering long after the night has left.
your kisses were shooting stars
burning, bright, and fleeting.

your hands on my throat left shadows like
those dancing in the glow of dim street-lamps.
our bodies twisted underneath my sheets like
swaying reeds under the starry night sky and

i think i'm still enamoured.

**D**

eternal truths

it was
in your kiss
although i didn't know its taste at first

hope that turned sour
as distance between us grew

lust that dwindled away
the longer we were apart

regret that strengthened
the more i thought about us

peace that bloomed
when i understood the truth

it was always
just a kiss

never anything more

**D**

it's ok

it's ok that you've been let down again
i say to myself gently.
steadily going through the motions of
eating, sleeping, studying, crying
while my heart goes through the motions of
tearing, healing, beating, breaking.

it's ok that you fell for another one of those guys
i say with a wry smile.
what else can i do carrying a past littered with
the same tattoos
the same eyes
the same pretty lies formed by
the same pretty lips?

it's ok that you thought he was different
i say, even though i know i was a fool.
an arm draped over the dip of my waist
under heavy covers and heavy sleep
and suddenly i was blinded.

it's ok to still want him
i say, as i remember him holding my hand.
a gentle grip despite him not knowing that
my dreams were intertwined with his fingers.

it's ok to still think about him,
i say, sitting alone in my room.
pillows perfumed with

sweat and sweetness
fickleness and youth
naivety and lost innocence.

it's ok to let him go,
i say, breathing the words into the silence.
quiet resignation telling me

he had never wanted to stay.

*flattery and flirtation*
*or*
*the one i loved drunkenly*

# C

ephemeral

words spilled out of your mouth and
lingered in the air
trapped in the moment they

floated

suspended on tiny clouds of half-materialised desires and
i yearned for them to stay

**C**

the endless expanse

it's funny how one night can feel like an eternity
time seemed to shift and stretch around us

i could see infinite possibilities

whisper-soft grazes of our fingers and lips
unspoken words glimmering in our eyes
secrets spilling out in every exhale and

i could have stayed in your embrace forever

# C

easy

it was nothing new
at least, not for me but
there's comfort in familiarity
isn't there?

a reminder of
things that never happened
words that were never spoken
feelings that were never acknowledged

a reminder of
everyone who came before you

**C**

your fiction

when did i become
nothing more
than a projection of your desires?

when did i become
nothing more
than a fleeting fantasy?

*half-formed lies, fully-broken promises*
*or*
*the one i loved unconditionally*

**R**

beginnings

"i like your face" you say
and i feel my heart flutter

**R**

into the fire

"you want to feel safe"

if that's the case
why do i want to be with you?

see
i don't think i want to feel safe
i think i just want to feel

i want to escape all this
numbness
and so

i'll fall into you

# R

clichés

orange juice without bits
a kiss on my lips
i'm losing my wits
with your hands on my hips

sounds like a bad pop song
right?

it felt like one too

**R**

lost in time

i liked us when we were uncomplicated
when movies, kisses, playlists, and mints
were all we were and
all we thought we could be

it was simple
like the words that left your mouth
the compliments you stated like facts
the promises you never dreamt of breaking

why did it have to change?

**R**

too little, too slow

words keep getting stuck in your throat like
thoughts keep getting lodged in my mind

funny how
in a world intent on instant communication
we love in a series of delays

# R

blinded

i never set out to replace her
you know that, right?
sometimes i think you get it
other times
you're so clueless

**R**

imaginary

were you telling the truth?

not the time you told me
you liked me
i could feel that even through all my denial and
i'm sure
you knew it too

i mean
all the times you talked about them
the others

sometimes it felt like
you were lying to me but
other times?

it felt like
i was lying to myself

**R**

don't we want more?

it's unfair to expect so much when
you give so little

too little of you
to make me feel sure
too little of you
to prove you care

nothing of you
to show you'll stay

**R**

a disappointing reality

"love" never was said aloud
at least
not in the way i wanted

you said
"love you"
flippantly
carelessly
callously
like it was a joke that rolled off your tongue
as easily as every word that came before

**R**

bitter confessions

the first time you told me
you loved me
it wasn't romantic or earth-shattering or beautifully cliché
it was
confusing

it should have been a moment of
security
permanence
connectivity
but i'd never before felt so unsure
i'd never before felt so alone

i knew you weren't serious
a chuckle escaped your lips and
i knew it then like
i know it now

you would never love me
the way i dreamed you would

you would never love me
the way i thought you could

**R**

and so the dream fades

you got into the wrong side of the bed
trivial, right?
i swallowed down the lump in my throat

"that's my side"

you laughed, pulled me closer

"no, don't you remember? i always take this side.
have you already forgotten?"

but i hadn't
how could i forget anything about you
about us?

you'd complained about the lamp
you'd shifted and sighed and tossed and turned all night
so i'd offered to switch

from then on
that was your side.

but looking at you
smiling at me

you don't remember that night at all.

**R**

the gifts i couldn't give

i gave you more of myself than i've ever given them

you might not believe it but
every moment i spent with you was
more intimate
more important
than any amount of hours i ever spent with them

i tried to tell you but
you wouldn't listen
you couldn't hear anything i said because
to you
all that mattered was everything i did with them
i could never do with you

all that mattered was what i couldn't give you

and so i started to wonder if
the parts of me that were left
were already too broken to be desired

**R**

new

you don't cut me with your words
you don't bruise me with your actions
you don't haunt me with your presence but

you wound me with your absence.

you see
you hurt me softly, slowly
surely.

it's never been brutal
nor biting
it just aches
the way an old wound would if it were prodded and
poked until it reopened.

pain's funny that way.

**R**

exposed

i lost my sanctuary
when i lost you

you offered to be there for as long as i needed but
when need turned into want
you left

i wish i knew why

**R**

end scene

it's as if one day
you flicked a switch
as easily as that
we were done

a blackout
everything disappeared but
while i was suddenly blinded
you were content to just
stay in the dark

**R**

how futile

"i miss you"
i breathe into the night
knowing full well you'll never hear
hoping you might just the same

**R**

clarity

i wish i would have known
you'd always choose her

that's never going to change but
you hate hearing that
don't you?

# R

role reversal

missed calls
unanswered texts
funny how i decide to
draw     the     line
when you decide you're ready to step
closer

**R**

irreparable

no one tells you that puzzle pieces break.

they snap, splinter, stop fitting together
what once used to be perfect
suddenly becomes uncomfortable.

try as you might to
fix it
ignore it
adjust it
accept it

you can't.

you'll never be able to.

**R**

a fragmented picture

it's hard to complete one another
when you're both already broken.

we found that out too late
didn't we?

**R**

never built for compromise

when i asked for space
you held me tighter
when i asked for more
you disappeared

you always were too much
or too little
you never once tried
to meet me halfway

i wonder why that is

**R**

the cracks remain

you broke me apart
pieced me back together
but
as gentle as your hands were
i still don't feel whole

**R**

poorly scripted

"i don't want to be another bad story"

i read your words on the screen
smiled through my tears
i believed you then and
i believe you now

you never wanted to be a bad story but
that's what you became

**R**

our somethings were nothing to you

we could've had something you know
not everything
just something

but even something would have been enough for me

**R**

the story of us

we were on the cusp of something
weren't we?
something bigger than the both of us
something we had a taste of but could never fully achieve

only
stories like ours are predetermined
destined to be
nearlys
maybes
almosts

*filling the void*
*or*
*the one i loved momentarily*

**A**

playing catch

caught your eye
caught my breath
caught these feelings
oh

just another boy
throwing words around like
they're nothing

but
they're something to me

ridiculous, i know

**A**

fading memories

everyone focuses on the meet cute but

i don't remember how we met
too-strong drinks, dim lights, overwhelming loneliness
in the midst of it
you were there

i don't remember what i said to you
not the first thing nor the last but
snippets of our conversation float through my mind like
newspaper clippings or a jammed dictaphone

i don't remember who you were
not the superficial things
your name, your face, your story, those all stuck but
the more i think about you the less real you feel

i don't remember where you went
alternating between silhouettes and cigarettes
it felt like i lost you but maybe
you never wanted to be found

i don't remember why we kissed
just that we did but

that's the one part
i want to forget

**A**

a minute or more

i didn't know it then and
you don't know it now but
what we shared was more than
a sloppy, toothy, smiling kiss
at 1:27am
in the middle of a crowded bar

if only i knew how to tell you

**A**

unhealthy, isn't it?

i spent hours crying in that bar
in your bar, i guess

a strawberry fizz please
can you make it double strength?
oh, ok
never mind

he approached you but spoke to me
i was angry, tearful, so so hurt but
he didn't notice
they never do

no, i don't want you to buy me a drink
i want you to leave me alone.

a shot of tequila please
where's the salt?
perfect -
wow, that lime was sour

they're loud, rowdy
annoying, to be frank
i'm reaching boiling point or melting
i really can't tell

a triple vodka and cranberry please
is that allowed?
it doesn't matter

i need it either way

i sipped it slowly
but it hit me hard

i looked you in the eye
you smiled blankly, professionally
like you've been taught to do
like those four hours had never happened

my lips were loose
my heart too
i felt it rattling around my chest when i asked you
do you remember me?

"vaguely"

a slow blink, a casual nod
i walk away with a resigned smile

i'm getting good at this

## A

i know you

i think you're lying
when you say
you don't remember me

maybe that's
arrogance
maybe that's
hope
maybe that's
something else entirely
but

i believe your smile
more than your words
i believe your eyes
more than your actions

is that so wrong of me?

**A**

anyone but me

it's funny how you tell me

"i'm not looking for anything serious"

that's not the truth
is it?
you just aren't looking for anything serious
with me

because it's been
one month
one week
one day
since i was with you and
you're already in her bed

because it's been
one night
since i was with you and

she's already in your heart

*unfulfilled fantasies*
*or*
*the one i loved mistakenly*

**L**

and we'll build gardens in the sky

forget castles in the sky
let me build us a garden

let me create an eden far removed from
this earth

an earth where we aren't together.

let flowers bloom, let trees take root
let streams flow, let birdsong swell
let everything live beautifully, harmoniously
openly

openly the way we'll never be able to.

**L**

certainties

there's something comforting about the fact
we're nothing alike

me and her, i mean

she's not a better -me-
just a different -she-

and that's a lot easier to deal with

it's ok, you know?
i've made my peace with it

i love me

you love she

neither of those things should ever change

# You
## and
# Me

*our greatest tragedy*
*or*
*the way i love too freely*

**You**

waking up

there's nothing wrong with
the way i look
the way i think
the way i love

why did you convince me otherwise?

**You**

you're all the same

i swallowed the lies
you pressed against my mouth and
i wondered
why they tasted so sweet

**You**

give me something concrete

sometimes
i love the thought of love
sometimes
i love the thought of you

but
what use is
love in abstractions

**Future You**

how i choose to love

i fell in love with you before i knew you
typical, right?
like half the world before me and
half the world after me

my feelings aren't all that special
at least
not from your point of view

it's just
to me
they're everything
to me
you're everything

**Me**

defining heartbreak

i've never been in love.

hard to believe
isn't it?

countless poems
countless encounters
countless nights in countless arms
but
i've never known love
at least
not in the way i'd like

i thought i loved them once
gave them parts of me
i swore were sacred
gave them time and energy
i should have kept for myself
but
giving can't be mistaken for loving
at least
not in the way i'd believed

i've been with people
numerous people
in intimate ways
in casual ways
in ways perhaps i shouldn't have
but

none of them were really there
at least
not in the way i'd hoped

i've wanted people
wished for them even
some superficially
some deeply
a few wholly
but
they never wanted permanence
at least
not in the way i'd offered

see
what's heartbreak to me?
it's disappointment.

i've never loved and lost
but
i've often lost before i've even loved

isn't that somehow sadder?

**Me**

chasms

how many ways can i articulate regret and
how long will it take for my heart to understand

## Me

rewriting fairytales

everything i'd believed to be fate
was merely just
coincidence

**Me**

no more

i gave my body to strangers
in the hope i'd feel warmth

how wrong i was

PERISH BLOOM WITHER PERISH BLOOM WITHER PERISH BLOOM WITHER PERISH BLOOM WITHER PERISH BLOOM WITHER PERISH BLOOM WITHER PERISH BLOOM WITHER PERISH BLOOM WITHER PERISH BLOOM

## Me

natural decay

then
i watched flowers bloom
in vases and in my mind

now
i watch those same flowers
wither and perish